THE CAREGIVER'S BEATITUDES

ROBERT MARTIN

Energion Publications
Gonzalez, FL
2014

Cover Design: Henry Neufeld

ISBN10: 1-63199-056-X
ISBN13: 978-1-63199-056-4

Energion Publications
P. O. Box 841
Gonzalez, FL 32560
850-525-3916

energion.com
pubs@energion.com

TABLE OF CONTENTS

INTRODUCTION

In the summer of 2012, my wife and I began a rather interesting journey together. And by "interesting" I mean the same sort of "interesting" that is implied in the ancient apocryphal Chinese curse "May you live in interesting times." You see, my wife was diagnosed in July 2012 with (to use the medical, techno-geeky terminology) Type II invasive ductal carcinoma. For those of you less involved in the whole process, this is breast cancer.

This put me in a role which I don't think I really have ever excelled at. I'm the big strong daddy, the strong and determined husband. I'm the intellectual, the rational, the factual person. I'm the one who thrives on logic and reasonable, predictable progression. Emotions need to be subject to the mind. Me? Give compassionate, loving, gentle care to someone dealing with a serious illness? Don't make me laugh.

And yet, that is where I found myself. My choice was reduced, then, not to whether I'd be a caregiver, but more what kind of caregiver I'd be. This had been a serious wrestling point for me as it was entirely new territory and way beyond my comfort zone. I searched and sought for some sort of set of guiding principles of what this should look like for me. As an Anabaptist, I gravitated to the Sermon on the Mount in Matthew 5-7, as that, traditionally, has been the set of values for Anabaptists for centuries. The Beatitudes immediately stood out to me and I started meditating on them. The more I pondered them, the more I saw them as not just a general description of what members of the Kingdom of Heaven should be like, but how they could be applied to this role as a caregiver. I invite you, then, to walk along with me in exploring these little bits of truth and living with them as applications for being a caregiver. May this journey be a blessing to you.

CHAPTER 1
POOR IN SPIRIT

B LESSED are the poor in spirit, for theirs is the kingdom of heaven. (Matthew 5:3)

First of all, this word "blessed" is rather unfortunately used in a lot of translations of the Bible. It really is not in common use today and, where it is, it usually means "good fortune" and "health and wealth" and all that sort of stuff. I've seen some translations that replace it with the word "happy" which also just doesn't seem to do justice to what is represented in the Beatitudes. I don't think anyone "poor in spirit" or "persecuted" can be said to be "happy" by most people. So I turned to the Amplified Bible (since I'm not a Greek scholar) to find out what others have to say about what this word means.

> *Blessed (happy, to be envied, and spiritually prosperous—with life-joy and satisfaction in God's favor and salvation, regardless of their outward conditions) are the poor in spirit (the humble, who rate themselves insignificant), for theirs is the kingdom of heaven!* (Matthew 5:3, AMP)

While the Amplified version expands the word "blessed" to mean "happy," it expands upon it to express something that's deeper than just a surface satisfaction with circumstances. There is a characteristic of joy and contentment with God and his plans, even if the stuff going on around us seems so stupid and horrendous. This is important to remember as we go through the Beatitudes. "Blessed" is a state of mind similar to what James mentions when he calls people to "consider it pure joy" (James 1:2), that the circumstances of life, difficult as they currently are, will lead to something better down the road and this hope is the source of our deep satisfaction.

When Jesus says "Blessed are the poor in spirit," he's calling his listeners to a hope that goes beyond what is happening right here and now. There's something coming down the road that will make the current circumstances all seem a distant memory. But what does it mean to be "poor in spirit"?

The Amplified Version calls "poor in spirit" those who are humble or see themselves as insignificant. From the perspective of a caregiver, this doesn't seem to fit at first. I don't think any caregiver really feels that way. Caregivers realize how important and significant their role is and that significance is probably the biggest source of stress. We feel like the weight of the world is on us, that everything we do has massive consequences, and the slightest slip will have a devastating impact. Under this massive weight, we mere humans feel like we just don't have the strength. There is no amount of spirited attitude which will bear up against the pounding of all the waves of adversity and trials and troubles. "Poor in spirit" is more than just a simple sense that we are lesser beings. "Spiritual poverty" is what the New Century Version calls it. "Realize they need God" is how the New Living Translation terms it. This "poor in spirit" is a massive surrender that realizes, as important as a caregiver is, mere mortal human strength and power is insignificant to deal with this mess of stuff that assaults us constantly. We despair and wonder how in the world can we have any sort of joy in this?

The promise of this Beatitude is that these horrendously, spiritually crushed people will receive the Kingdom of Heaven. But what does this mean? To answer that, we need to know what Jesus means by the Kingdom of Heaven. The Kingdom of Heaven is where strangers put salve on the wounds of their enemy and pay for their care at the local inn (ref. Matthew 10:25-37). The Kingdom of Heaven is where storms are calmed, demons are cast out, illnesses are healed, and the poor and oppressed are encouraged. This is all good "Bible" stuff but, when you're down in the depths of this spiritual poverty, what you want to know is how it impacts right here, right now.

In all of the things about the Kingdom of Heaven, both in the gospels and in the later epistles, one thing comes out pretty clear. The Kingdom of Heaven is not a place where you are alone. People take care of people. The gifts and talents given by God to the people in that Kingdom are there for the many and varied purposes in caring for each other, helping each other, lifting each other up and encouraging each other to keep going. The spiritual poverty of the lonely caregiver is met with the lavish spiritual wealth of the community of believers. There is a certain sense of the future when everything will be fixed, but at the same time we have the Kingdom among us here and now. This is how God blesses the poor in spirit. He has provided them with this space full of people who are bound together by this sense of mutual care and support, driven by this insanely huge love that drives them to "value others above yourself" (Philippians 2:3-4). The very same drive that pushes the caregiver to give up their own ambitions and agenda for their loved one is the drive that puts the Kingdom people in place to take care of them.

For the caregiver who feels the weight of responsibility of the care for their loved one and, especially in a case like mine where the loved one is a spouse, of doing all those things that they previously did, pure joy comes not from some sense of individual strength. The blessing comes from that group of people around caregivers who are walking along with them, driven by the same Spirit of God that inspires care for a loved one with an intense, sacrificial love. Caregivers are not alone in their journey. They are the pinnacle of a pyramid of people. All these people behind them, lifting them up, supporting them, each one also being lifted up and supported, and so on. And supporting all of them, as a network of webbing, binding them all together, is this spiritual love that comes only from God. This is the Kingdom of Heaven promised to the poor in spirit.

FIRST STEPS:

Here are some practical things that I've started doing to find that joy in my spiritual poverty.

1) It is pretty wonderful to read the Psalms of David, especially those that were written during the trying times. Psalm 22 is one of my favorites. Especially look at those psalms that have

promises based upon what others have received. Read the psalms and remember who God is and where he is.

2) Pray, pray, pray ... and when all else fails, pray again. This is always my personal struggle point as my mind gets easily distracted when I try to pray. But when you get "poor in Spirit" you need to be refilled. And the best way to do that is to go to the source and spend time drinking in what is available at the source of the Spirit: love, joy, peace, patience, kindness, goodness, faithfulness, gentleness and self-control (Galatians 5:22-23).

3) Gather some prayer partners. I learned during my time in seminary that having a small group of people praying for you can lend wonderful support. Find a few friends who are absolute confidants, people that you can trust with your deep soul. Pour out all your junk to them so that they can pick you up and lift you up to God.

4) Drop the pride. I'm stubborn in that I want to do things on my own. When you're under a ton of weight, though, you can't. You need help. Go looking for help and, when someone offers it, don't turn it down. Let them be God's blessing to you and remember, they too will be blessed as God uses them to be his hands and feet.

CHAPTER 2
MOURNING

BLESSED are those who mourn, for they will be comforted. (Matthew 5:4)

To reflect on mourning as a caregiver while the person being cared for is still alive seems morbid. In my own journey, I had the same thought. Even at the time, I realized that my wife would certainly survive the treatments for the cancer (and she did and is thriving). I knew I was going to have her around for a long time to come. This was something to celebrate. She was cancer-free following the initial surgery. Shouldn't I have been partying and happy? What did mourning have to do with me?

Those of you who have relatives who are going through cancer treatments or other long illness and are caregivers yourselves know that it's not quite this easy. The role of a caregiver is a hard journey with the need for a lot of strength, patience, and endurance. And during this time, you will end up losing some things that are precious to you, even if only for a time. The Message paraphrase of this Beatitude describes it as feeling "like you've lost what is most dear to you." During my own time as a caregiver, even with a positive outlook, there were some things that I felt like I had lost or was about to lose.

My wife didn't have the energy necessarily to be my wife sometimes. There were times when things were going well. However, before her surgery and immediately afterwards, my wife was focused on the fatigue and pain she was experiencing. I had to step back a bit and let her heal and regain her strength. As much as I love her, this is hard to do. And it didn't end there. The continuing medical treatments brought about their own effects of pain and exhaustion. I mourned losing the intimate connection with my wife during this time.

Our lives had been turned upside down, backwards, inside out, sideways, and totally topsy-turvy over the course of my wife's illness. We had a rhythm to our life with school, work, family, and so on. It was so comfortable to know what was coming up and to have some control over what we did and when we did it. But this was no longer the case. It was like the cancer had taken over not just my wife's body but our entire lives. Everything was scheduled around doctor's appointments, tests, treatment schedules, etc. My wife's illness coincided with the holiday seasons and we realized that those deeply treasured family times would be impacted by cancer treatments and side effects. I mourned the loss of our "normal" lives.

My daughters (ages 9 and 12 at the time) had been wonderful during this time. They had an amazing understanding and compassion for their mother, doing whatever was asked of them with little complaint and with a glad heart as they helped out with things around our home. It was obvious, though, that the events in our lives were impacting them as well. They lost some innocence 5 years before when their beloved grandmother passed away suddenly. They had to face the serious illness of a loved one at such a young age. And now their mother was also seriously ill. I wish that children did not have to be exposed to such things in their lives. I mourned the loss of childhood innocence.

Silly as it may seem, I love my wife's hair. It was one of those little things when we were courting and during our marriage that has always been so much fun, to see the different ways, over the years that she's worn her hair and the playfulness about her when it comes to hairstyles and the like. We planned to have fun with hats and scarves during the chemotherapy treatments. And yet, I mourned the impending loss of my wife's crowning glory.

My wife was sick. This was a stark truth that I had to face. She is my other half, my better self. She completes me. Without her, I'm less than half what I could be. Before we married, I thought I was whole. But since we've been married, I realize how incomplete I was before. But then she fell ill and would be ill for some time before our journey's end. This was not how I wanted things to be. I wanted my wife to be healthy, to be energetic, to have a whole body, and to not have to go through the stress and trouble and trial of radiation and chemotherapy. I mourned my wife's health.

During this time in our lives, there were more things that came up that I mourned. But this gives a glimpse into what mourning means to a caregiver.

The Beatitudes tell us in the NIV translation that those who mourn will be comforted. But, again, our modern language weakens that term a bit. It brings to mind people sending flowers, reciting platitudes, and even quoting the dreaded scripture "All things work for good ..." (Romans 8:28). As true as that scripture may be, when you are in that period of deep mourning, it is rarely helpful. Again, I turn to The Message paraphrase to help me with finding that "pure joy." The Message doesn't say "comfort," it talks about being able to be "embraced by the One most dear to you" (Matthew 5:4).

This is the comfort that Jesus promises during mourning. There is so much that I lost or was losing in my time as a caregiver. All those comfort points were being knocked away. There was nothing to cling to of certainty any more in this world. For the caregiver, though, comfort comes from grabbing hold of Jesus and crying tears of loss. In return, Jesus returns the favor and takes us up in his arms and just holds us. There is a spiritual comfort that comes when we cry out to Jesus. When we pour out our grief to him, the promise is that he can take it and absorb it, and just hold us in his peace and love.

On a more practical side, we cannot forget that Jesus has a very real body today as well. Paul frequently refers to the followers of Jesus as his Body. We, as Christians, are Jesus hands and feet and arms. With that in mind, when we think about being embraced by Jesus, we find that same embrace among our brothers and sisters in God's family. I know that sometimes caregivers feel the need to show a strong, sturdy presence to those in our care. But at some point in time, they need to feel some sort of support and comfort.

Caregivers cannot be afraid to be vulnerable. In my own journey, I have found immense comfort in crying on someone's shoulder and just pouring out my grief and simply having that person receive it. They give simply an embrace and a gentle presence. There is an intense contentment and joy to lean into someone's arms with the depth and darkness of mourning and just feel it all melt away in love.

Blessed are those who mourn. Jesus is waiting with open arms to embrace and comfort you. Jesus' friends and followers add to that spiritual embrace with the beautiful gift of presence.

FIRST STEPS:

1) Take some time alone to go off somewhere and just cry to God. My wife didn't need me around 24/7, as much as I may have felt like I needed to be there. It's okay to take a little time to go off and grieve and to lean on God's love. Pour out your heart to him and, when it is all out, just lean and rest in the quiet for a time.

2) Psalm 23 is an amazing promise. In the valley of the shadow of death, in the presence of your enemies (illness, time schedules, etc), in the darkness of evil, Jesus is there as the good shepherd, giving his presence. Meditate on this daily to ingrain it in your being so that, in the dark moments, these promises will always be right there.

3) Find a confidant other than the loved one you are caring for. Your loved one doesn't need to be burdened with your own grief; they have enough of their own. Seek someone who will be there for you when all you need is the embrace of peace. Find someone a little thick-skinned that can take a beating. Mourning is a passionate thing and can get a little intense. Don't be afraid to be vulnerable to them and to just let it all out there. If God's Spirit is with them, they will return nothing but grace and peace to you.

CHAPTER 3
MEEKNESS

B LESSED are the meek for they will inherit the earth.
(Matthew 5:5)

It almost seems hypocritical to be writing about being meek. There is a lot of self-promotion that goes into writing with getting readers, promoting your writing, and getting the word out. And being meek does not seem to fit. "Self-effacing" and "humble" are two synonyms for meekness. It certainly does not seem to fit the world of writing to be meek.

But as a caregiver, it is something we are called to do. I found it to be an absolute necessity to set aside my own desires, my own wishes, my own preferences in order to care for my wife. When she was recovering from the lumpectomy, the things that I wanted for my own comfort took back burner in order to make sure she could focus on her recovery. This was a struggle for me at times. My needs, out of necessity, took second place. While I felt tired and worn out, I set myself aside for her out of love. I did this again during her chemotherapy regimen.

This is the meekness that Jesus was talking about. Of anyone in the history of the world, Jesus embodied this. Everything he did was sacrificially done for the good of others with his own needs taking second place. He was always stopping and talking to people. He healed blind beggars on his way to someplace "important." He bent down, both literally and figuratively, to serve those whom society had set aside as inconsequential. Don't get me wrong, my wife is anything but inconsequential to me. But the attitude of putting her first, above everything else, is modeled by Jesus. Biblical meekness is not being a doormat. Meekness is about loving someone so much that you completely forget yourself in the process.

Philippians 2:3-4 describes it like this:

Do nothing out of selfish ambition or vain conceit. Rather, in humility value others above yourselves, not looking to your own interests but each of you to the interests of the others.

This was not easy for me to do all the time and gets wearying, especially for an introvert like myself. I was challenged to find joy in that time of submission. I turned then, to the Beatitude for the promise. Jesus told his listeners that the meek will inherit the earth. To be honest, I don't want the planet. You can keep this dirty ball of rock. What good does a planet do me?

Jesus' words in this Beatitude echo the words of the psalmist in Psalm 37:

But the meek will inherit the land and enjoy peace and prosperity. (Psalm 37:11)

That psalm talks about enemies and about conquering and so on. Obviously, our loved one that we are caring for is not the enemy so how can we talk about submitting to the enemy so that, in the future, we'll have abundant peace?

But what if the enemy is myself, my own warring desires? What if that is where the true battle is? The cancer battle, as with many such battles, is a battle of flesh and blood, doctors and nurses, medicines and technology. For most caregivers, we are not qualified to fight that battle. We have a battle of heart and spirit to fight. In the last two chapters I wrote about being poor in spirit and about mourning the losses caregivers face and will face. These are also battles of the heart. Are these battles ones that can be won alone?

The answer is no. Psalm 37 talks about living faithfully to God, committing to His ways, living a righteous live before Him. But it is God who will win the battle. When it is all said and done, once the battle is won, then we will receive a peace that passes understanding. Caregivers can't win the fight. Instead of fighting, we simply submit. We need to take on an attitude of meekness and humility, submitting not just to the needs of our loved ones, but submitting our lives to God's purposes and principles. We need to hand over those warring desires to God, give them over to him, confess that we cannot do it on my own, and let God take care of it. This is what will bring that "pure joy" that James talks about concerning our trials (James 1:2).

There is no doubt that caregivers love their charges deeply. But, as caregivers, the personal desires cannot be held on to any more. Meekness is our model, given by Jesus. We need to give our desires to Him, no longer holding on to them. Our trust is then placed on Jesus to fill us with contentment and peace as we pour out our love, attention, and service to our loved ones. In the end, when the battles are done, both those in the bodies of our stricken loved ones as well as in our own souls, we can then sit back and enjoy the abundant peace that comes from doing what God has asked of us.

FIRST STEPS:

1) Sit down in the quiet somewhere and spend time going over all your desires, all the things you wish you could be doing, and pray a prayer of confession to God. Give each and every one of them over to him, asking him to conquer them in your soul, and to give you that peace that comes from doing what is right. Believe me, this is an amazing experience to be able to just let it all go. You may need to do it more than once, but each time there is that sense of peace and joy that comes along with it.

2) Read Psalm 37, but instead of looking at it as external enemies, look at it as your selfish side warring with your loving side. Meditate on what God promises to do for those who live rightly and center those promises in your life.

3) Speak words of love to your loved one, frequently, constantly, often. My wife is an independent sort and did not want to be an imposition or a burden on me. She needed to know that everything I was doing, as inconvenient as it may have seemed,

I did out of love for her. Tell your loved one this in words. Your actions certainly play it out, but sometimes they need to know that there is a deep love there so that they can also enjoy that abundant peace that comes through meekness.

CHAPTER 4
HUNGER AND THIRST

B LESSED are those who hunger and thirst for righteousness, for they will be filled. (Matthew 5:6)

Did you ever get hungry? I mean, really hungry where you feel your stomach cramping to the point that it is excruciatingly painful and you look at scraps of food on the ground around a dumpster and actually contemplate eating it? A hunger where you would almost kill for a slice of bread, no matter how dry and stale it is?

Or have you been thirsty where your lips so dry they are bleeding, you can't swallow because your throat is so dry it is swelling shut, and your skin so dry that it cracks and peels painfully?

Yeah, me neither.

What I described above is what is really meant by being hungry and thirsty when Jesus talks about it. This is not just a little twinge of "Oh, it's dinner time" or that little bit of dryness where you crack open a can of soda and take a swig to satisfy it. The hunger and thirst Jesus is talking about in the fourth Beatitude is an intense desire for being filled that is excruciating and painful to the extreme. It is a life or death sort of thing.

The hunger and thirst is not for physical food though. Many translations use the word "righteousness," others use "justice." Neither of those words is very helpful in our culture because the first brings up images of piety and morality and sinless living and the other brings up (depending upon your view) either images of retribution for wrongs done or correction of social ills. The word used is much deeper than that. Again, turning to The Amplified Bible, we see that it has to do with "uprightness and right standing with God."

But as a caregiver, what does the hunger and thirst for this right relationship have to do with the daily struggle of caring for a loved one who is seriously ill? That right standing just seems so

15

hyper-spiritual and just doesn't seem to connect at all with the reality of a caregiver. For me, I was more worried about my wife's pain management after her surgery than I was whether or not I was praying enough every day. During the chemo regimen, I was preoccupied with my wife's strength and nutrition and with the weakness and frailty from the medicines she received. At the same time, I worried about keeping her spirits up, making sure that she felt loved, making sure that she had an ear to hear when she despaired and a shoulder to cry on when the tears came. All this Bible reading, praying, moral living kind of righteousness just didn't seem realistic in the face of these very human and mortal problems.

Caregivers perhaps, when they express this sort of sentiment, receive platitudes and pithy sayings like, "Man does not live by bread alone" and "Jesus is all you need." But reality is reality and the daily struggle for the caregiver is much more mundane. While I do not deny the spiritual side of my life, there is a saying that I've heard tossed around which goes something like "People cannot hear the gospel when their bellies are so loud from hunger." When reality intrudes in all its ugliness, it's hard to focus on those things that do not satisfy the more immediate problems. When the care of my beloved wife consumed my life, it was hard to take the time to seek God because of the intrusion of the painful facts of life.

Once again, the question is where do caregivers find that pure and confident joy alluded to by being called "blessed"? The promise in this beatitude is that those who hunger and thirst for the right relationship with God will be filled and satisfied. That when we hunger and thirst for right living we will find what we need. But it is more than that we will find it, it will be given to us to the point where we will no longer feel the need. We will be completely satisfied and filled.

This is a message of grace and hope to the caregiver. Being hungry and thirsty for righteousness implies that we are not satisfied yet. There will come a time when we will be, a time when we'll be able to fill that spiritual belly with the good food of God. There will come a time when we will be able to have the time and energy to do what we need to do in order to be satisfied from this hunger and thirst. God's promises are more than just what Mary Poppins calls "pie-crust promises." They are not easily made and then easily broken. It will happen.

In the meantime, this is not an excuse to do nothing. Even hungry and thirsty people eat a little and drink a little every day to survive. A caregiver may not find the satisfaction they desire, especially when exhaustion at the end of the day claims them. But they do need that little bit of spiritual food and drink every day. For me, I would turn off the radio during my hour commute to and from work and spend time talking to God. I would grab a quick snatch of scripture at work between tasks, getting little tastes of God's promises. I would sing along, loud and proud, to worship music on the radio, giving my praise while I could, much to the amusement of the other drivers on the road. No, they were not satisfying meals, but I was seeking God and hungering for more. God promised that I would be filled. At the time, the promise was enough. God understands and he will give caregivers what they need to serve, when they need to serve, specifically at their loved one's side, supporting and strengthening them.

FIRST STEPS:

1) I gave some examples above of ways that I found to get my "little snacks" every day. It took a bit of time for me to find these as I was blinded by having to have all or nothing. But once I found one, I found it easier to find more. Look at your daily schedule and see where you can find those little bites of time to seek after God's wisdom and purpose.

2) Read Isaiah 55. This passage from Isaiah highlights the importance and greatness of God's wisdom and purpose. It is a great reminder of the need we have for God's wisdom and the importance of making it a priority, even when reality intrudes.

3) Don't be so hard on yourself. You have an important job right now, caring for a loved one. This is where God has called you

right now and God is gracious enough to give you that time and space to do what you need to do. Your satisfaction will come in time.

CHAPTER 5
MERCY

B LESSED are the merciful, for they will be shown mercy.
(Matthew 5:7)

This book started out as a series of articles on my internet blog. As I sat down to write this reflection on the Beatitude of mercy, I drew a blank. I really wasn't able to figure out how I could apply mercy to my role as a caregiver. But something happened that day which really brought it into focus for me. God reached down, moved someone, and now I know what it means to be shown mercy.

First of all, let's set aside some of the popular views of mercy. Mercy is not putting someone out of their misery. "Mercy killing" is what some people think of when they hear the word mercy. Mercy is also not setting aside a deserved punishment, at least not by itself. Sometimes this is done to gain points with observers. "Oh, look at him, isn't he merciful?" Being the movie buff that I am, to hear that word, "merciful," conjures up images of Maximus and Commodus in the 2000 movie, Gladiator.

But when it comes to the biblical term of mercy, it is more than just commuting a punishment or relieving pain. It goes deeper than that. Some of the translations I read in preparing this reflection used the word "kindness." I would suggest that "compassion" is another way of putting it. The Bible many times refers to God's "lovingkindness" as the King James Version puts it when talking about God's amazing love. Psalm 117 actually uses the term "merciful kindness." So there is something about mercy that involves love and kindness. It's a bigger concept than just a relief of pain, suffering, or judgment.

As a caregiver during my wife's recovery, my days were spent exercising kindness in immense quantities. Refilling ice-packs, refilling water bottles, getting pillows, helping her get out of the chair, bringing her a meal, etc., all came under this immense kindness. Giving her a hug when she felt defeated also counted. Lending an ear when the constant litany of doctor's appointments and tests weighed her down goes a long way to showing this biblical form of mercy. This is probably one of the biggest roles a caregiver can fill, to give that constant no restrictions, no compromising, totally sold-out, multi-faceted mercy and love to your loved one.

But I realized one day that I was insufficient. Breast cancer is not just a disease for some women. It is a violation of them being a woman. A primary physical characteristic that defines her woman-hood had been damaged. Her femininity had been attacked. Along with that, chemotherapy was going to destroy another characteristic of her womanhood. Her hair would be gone and she would no longer have that thing, that physical characteristic with which she could express herself.

All the tests and doctors' appointments and such made her feel not like a female human being but as a thing to be poked and prodded. It began to feel like a violation. The fatigue of medicines and tests and such would drain her of any feeling of being beau-tiful and valued and loved, not that physical characteristics are of paramount importance, but it was a matter of self-esteem and self-worth. These are things that, as a man, I could only understand in a purely clinical sense. My mercy is limited in that I could not meet the emotional needs of this wonderful woman because I am simply not a woman.

I didn't realize this, really, until I got an offer that day via a Facebook message from a distant relative and friend. We had con-nected through that magic of Facebook where you find friends that are friends of other friends. That morning, her message contained a question as to whether or not my wife would enjoy a time of pam-pering, compliments of her and Mary Kay cosmetics. This friend is a woman (not sure if there are men who are Mary Kay consultants, but kudos to them if there are), a nurse, and a cosmetological ex-pert. When she asked me this, I realized here was someone who could give my wife something that I had no hope of doing, the kindness of a woman helping her feel like a woman again.

This blessed me. It's hard to describe exactly what happened in my heart. Matters of the heart are rarely easy to put into words. But it was like a weight which I didn't even know I was carrying was suddenly lifted off my back and I could stand up straight again. I didn't realize how much I needed that type of kindness until it was given to me. Just when I needed it, God's Spirit moved. I don't know what prompted this friend to offer what she did. What whisper did she hear? What nudge did she feel? What song or verse or word did she experience that moved her to message me with that offer? I don't know. I honestly don't need to know. It was enough to know that a kindness I did not seek was offered when I needed it, before I even knew I needed it.

God is good, all the time. When it seems like life around us is so horrible, so depressing, God is good. In the good times and the bad times, God is good. As we pour out God's goodness to others, God is faithful and will pour it back into us. My kindness to my wife had not gone unnoticed. As a caregiver, I knew that I will not be left empty. That mercy and love that I gave to my wife had been poured back into me to the point of overflowing. God is good, all the time.

FIRST STEPS:

1) Psalm 63 is an excellent reminder that God's love is better than life itself. Read it and meditate on what it means to be filled with God's "lovingkindness," even when it seems like you are empty.

2) When those little blessings come in, give thanks to God for them. God is not silent and distant, but he is moving and working around you and will move people to pour out kindness into your own life.

3) Don't turn away gifts offered in good grace. Pride sometimes gets in the way as we say, "I can do this on my own." As I mentioned in an earlier meditation, we cannot do this on our own. We need

others in our life to lift us up, support us, and even do those things that we just can't do on our own. Every little gift given is a way for God to give us the mercy that we need.

CHAPTER 6
PURE IN HEART

B LESSED are the pure in heart, for they will see God.
(Matthew 5:8)

Heart purity, as it is commonly dealt with in the world of Christianese, is concerned with those topics of moral and spiritual purity. Watch what you watch, don't listen to that devil music, make sure you stay away from these books, don't harbor anger in your heart, watch the selfish attitudes and motivations, don't lust, don't hate, and "be careful little eyes/ears/hands," etc. The goal of all this is to keep the heart clean and unsullied and ready to approach God. If you get all these rules in order, you will be able to get close to God, hence the beatitude's promise of "they will see God." But there are problems with this way of looking at things.

The first problem is how this can turn into a rules-oriented legalistic religion. Purity of life is important, but at the same time, it is not something that can be done on our own but something that we desperately need the cleansing power of God and God's Spirit working in us. It's not for no reason that the psalmist asks God to "create in me a clean heart" (Psalm 51:10).

Secondly, for the caregiver, this approach to heart purity really does not seem to apply. To be truthful, as much as we need this kind of moral purity, caregivers are so drawn into caring for their loved one that many of those temptations just don't really play a role. Drinking? I can't be drunk because I need to be able to do the driving to and from cancer treatments. Anger? How can I be angry and mad and hateful? I don't have the energy to waste on that stuff while I'm helping to care for two children and help my wife through her daily routines. Lust? It is hard to lust when you are confronted with blood and gore and bandages and vomit and tears. This puts a damper on the libido, you know?

No, for the caregiver, the heart purity that we desperately seek is something that sometimes seems so elusive. With every test, every procedure, every treatment, every surgery comes a whole host of possible complications and side effects and long term problems. These things are very real to us. Our loved one going through it all is facing, every time, the possibility of something going horribly wrong. And we are right there with them all the way. How can we not be when, at least in my case, it was my Better Half going through it? If the horrible thing was going to happen, it would have happened to both of us, not just her. Notice that I did not use the word "when" in that previous statement but, instead, used "if." This is the heart purity that caregivers seek. Caregivers seek a confidence that there is a God that loves them and doesn't really want the horrible things to happen. And with all the documentation, the noise of "this side effect" and "that possible outcome" and so on, it is so hard to focus on "God is good."

As a caregiver, our loved one needs us to be there with those words of comfort, to keep those words of fear and terror at bay and speak words of peace to them. Yes, reality must be dealt with, but at the same time my wife needed to be able to focus on healing and staying healthy through it all and dwelling on the negatives was no way to do that. I needed to be able to be that reminder that there is a good God. I needed to be able to hear her fears and return with confidence and peace. It was extremely difficult to do this when I was fighting the same fears and uncertainties.

This beatitude promises, though, that this purity of heart, on dwelling on the good things of God, would allow me to actually see God. This does not mean that I would actually see the dude with the white beard riding on a cloud or anything. Instead, if I'm focusing on the good things of God, just like if I'm focusing on a star in the sky, or focusing on the words on a page, God will become that much clearer to me in the events and happenings of our lives. When I focus on God, God reveals the way that the right people enter our lives at the right time to tell us the right things we need to hear, right then and there. When I focus on God, I'll hear

His words of peace in the songs on the radio, in the words of the Psalms, and in the prayers of friends and family. When I focus on God and keep that purity of remembering God's goodness, that is when God really becomes real and I can see who He is so much more clearly. When I seek that purity of heart where it is unsullied by doubts and fears and worries, then the beauty and goodness and *shalom* of God becomes so real, I can see God.

FIRST STEPS:

1) My wife made it a point to seek out God's promises to remember and meditate on throughout our journey. Filling your life and mind with those things make it so that there is no room for anything else. I've mentioned several times to seek through the Psalms for such words. This is an excellent practice and I've started really looking for the Psalms that speak those words of God's goodness. Paul says in Philippians 4:8-9 that when we focus on those good things, then God's goodness will become clear.

2) Don't deny the reality of the medicine and treatments. But when you've made the decisions and stuff, put it away. Don't get them out and read them anymore, don't dwell on them, don't listen to them anymore. These are not things to dwell on. The bad news, if it comes, won't be held off by worrying about it. Jesus tells us, "Tomorrow has enough troubles. Deal with today" (Matthew 6:34).

3) Seek God in prayer for that purity. Spend time with Him and pour out your fears and worries to Him. Release them to God and give up worrying about them. Pray for God to take away the darkness of the terror of "what if" and replace it with the peace of "God is."

CHAPTER 7
PEACEMAKER

B LESSED are the peacemakers, for they will be called children of God. (Matthew 5:9)

The notion of peace has great traction in the world today. Everyone seems to be saying "we need peace" and "pray for peace." There are two ways that it is viewed generally.

Peace is sometimes seen as the absence of conflict. People don't fight any more, people get along, there's no arguing, no hatred, everyone can live together and not rub each other the wrong way. Peace means no more fighting. And, to some extent, this is right. However, this is a little more shallow than the biblical peace to which Jesus calls people. Jesus was called the Prince of Peace and yet He stirred up conflict all over the place so we know that there's something else going on here.

The other way that peace is viewed is a sense of calm, of quiet, of tranquility. There is no noise, there is no chaos, and everything is smooth. A peaceful river is one that just flows gently. A peaceful forest is quiet except for bird song and the gentle rustling of breezes in the trees. Again, there is some of this in biblical peace but it is incomplete by itself.

The peace that is the peace of God is usually expressed by the Jewish word *shalom*. It is a complete wholeness that comes from living the way God intends and desires us to live. This may bring us into conflict with the world around us where our lifestyle challenges the status quo and makes others uncomfortable and threatened. This goes against that first perception of peace. However, if we are living rightly with others, doing what we can, as much as we are capable, to live at peace with them then this is what is required of us. We are at *shalom* even if others are not. It is certainly not tranquil and quiet and gentle sometimes as, when we challenge the status quo, it stirs up noise.

That is the peace that Jesus asks people to make. The Amplified Bible actually adds "maintain" to this verse as well to indicate that this peacemaking isn't just a once and done thing, but it is an ongoing process. We are asked not just to help bring *shalom* into the world, but to help maintain *shalom* wherever we are.

Enter the caregiver again. I know for a fact that a life that involves cancer treatments certainly does not feel peaceful, at least by the world's standards. I'm pretty confident the same holds true for any serious or long-term illness. During our cancer journey together, my wife and I saw five different doctors and who knows how many nurses and other technicians in a complicated, confusing web of care providers, services and procedures. With two active children, trying to schedule all those appointments around their school schedules as well as my own work schedule and my wife's routines was certainly not a peaceful endeavor as it turned our "status quo" upside down and inside out. Figuring out finances as we ended up with extra expenses for gas and other things related to the care certainly, in our current economy, did not give one a feeling of calm and tranquility. And chemotherapy and radiation therapy just added extra layers of complexity to things. Be a peacemaker? God seemed to ask the impossible.

The promise that goes along with this beatitude, on the surface, just doesn't seem practical at all in the face of the stresses of being a caregiver. What does being a child of God have to do with this? Aren't I that already?

Then I remembered something: God doesn't ask *shalom* of us because He wants to give us an impossible task. God asks *shalom* of us because God is already in *shalom* with us. For it to really work, we need to be in *shalom* with Him. This is what a child does to their parent: they trust the parent. The implicit, innocent trust of a child is proverbial. There is no question that the parent will care for the child. Jesus, in the same Sermon on the Mount, reminds us not to worry. God thinks we're better than grass. If that's the case and grass is taken care of, why not us? He also reminds us, a little later on, that as good a father and caregiver as I was, God is even better and won't forget our needs. This is so hard to remember sometimes. God will take care of us. This is God's *shalom* towards us. As I filled my role as a caregiver, I could not be a peacemaker within my own situation if I did not accept this peace from God. Notice the promise again. The peacemaker will be called a child of God. This is not a "bonus" for being a peacemaker. Being a peacemaker is evidence of something I already am. When I am a peacemaker, this is evidence of my being God's child.

The peacemaking of the caregiver in relationship towards their loved one is something that will naturally grow out of their sense of *shalom* in their relationship with God. The person being cared for is going to have worries and fears that come from their situation. The caregiver's job is to help them find a sense of *shalom* when they wrestle with it themselves. As God's child, the caregiver can help their charge know this *shalom*, this sense of "rightness" in their life by living it out themselves in their own relationship. In this essential role of a caregiver, not only do they help make peace in the lives of their loved ones, the caregiver helps them maintain it. It seems like a hard burden to bear, but the caregiver's own sense of *shalom* comes from knowing God is there bearing it with them and they don't have to do it alone.

FIRST STEPS:

1) Read Matthew 6:25-34 and Matthew 7:9-11 and reflect on all the ways God has provided for you already. During our journey, I remembered that I had a job, I had insurance, we had a wonderful church family that cared for us in more than just the spiritual sense. We were blessed, and still are. God had provided in ways we could not imagine. Look around and consider what God has done.

2) Sometimes the burden does seem overwhelming, even when you remember these things. Seek out someone who you trust and unload on them. I sometimes felt guilty doing so because it seemed almost like trying to garner sympathy and coerce them

into helping. But a good friend will always be there to give an ear and a shoulder. Take advantage of it. You don't have to stand alone.

CHAPTER 8
PUT TO FLIGHT

B LESSED are those who are persecuted because of righteousness, for theirs is the kingdom of heaven. (Matthew 5:10)

This last chapter of my reflections on the Beatitudes has been
one that I've really tried to figure out how to apply as a caregiver.
As I mentioned in an earlier chapter, the Beatitudes are considered by many to be a description of the basic characteristics of a
follower of Jesus. Everything to this point seems to apply to life as
a caregiver. But persecution? After reading about Richard Wurmbrand and others like him, I really hesitate to call simple troubles
and trials "persecution." In the case of my wife's illness and the
issues surrounding what it means to be a caregiver to a loved one,
I certainly was not and still am not, by that standard, persecuted,
at least, certainly, not by human beings.

But then I did a Greek Lexicon search on the word "persecution" as it is in the original language. I found that there is a nuance
to the word that involves not just what we typically think about
persecution (death, torture, pain, oppression, etc) but an aspect I
hadn't thought about. If you look at Acts 8:1, you see the English
word "persecution" again. Behind it is a different Greek word but
it has a similar connotation as the one in Matthew 5. More than
just the act of physical harm, persecution in these Biblical passag-
es implies a chase, a pursuit, and that the people involved as the
"persecuted" have been put to flight.

This flight is more than just running away because people
disagree with them. These persecuted folks run away because their
lives are characterized by a right living that conforms to God's standard. Living out God's way puts them in conflict with the rest of
the world who, in turn, go after them to make their lives miserable
in the process. For some, this results in the torment and torture
that Wurmbrand experienced. For others, this results in going into

hiding and living their righteous life in secret. For still others, this pushes them out of where they are into another country, another city, someplace different where their right living can continue to spread even though they may have lost their homes and livelihood in the process. Persecutions are unpleasant and extremely uncomfortable and it is strange to say that such people are blessed.

Living a Christian way in the USA, trying to be righteous, I cannot say I'm persecuted. No one is busting down my door and dragging me out into the night to be beaten, abused, or killed. No one is forcing me to do things I don't want to do. No one is threatening my life or the lives of my family because of what I believe. All things considered, I have it pretty good, at least in regards to my relationships with other people.

But allow me to stretch this a little bit. There are times, honestly, when the burden becomes very, very difficult. During my wife's treatments, I had to do a lot of things for my wife and do a lot around the home of things that my wife would normally do because she just wasn't able.

Additionally, I had an emotional burden to bear. I've described several times these reflections as the crushing of the spirit, the empty feeling, the mourning that I felt at times, the struggle with peace and contentment, and just the general fears and frustrations that come with the never-ending litany of tests and doctor visits and treatment schedules and so on. And while I was doing all this, I was providing strength and comfort and support for my wife as she, too, was feeling almost the exact same things … and more.

Through all of it, I needed to keep it together. I needed to do what I was called to do out of love. I needed to be that strength, the confidence, that support for my family. I needed to be a witness to the rest of the world about the different kind of hope and contentment that followers of Jesus are supposed to have. Under all that pressure, I felt like I was being pursued and chased around by big, ugly, scary guys with bad teeth and tattoos on their eye-balls ready to do me bodily harm.

For you purists, no, this was not "persecution." But that temptation is there to just throw in the towel and run screaming into the night. We come back, now, to the Beatitude and the promise that God gives us. In this little bit of poetry, Jesus ties up the whole package by using the same blessing in this Beatitude as He did in the first. When the feeling like everything is coming at me, hunting me down around every corner, I have the promise that the Kingdom of Heaven is mine.

When it comes to the Kingdom of Heaven, there is a very important piece of information to remember. Every kingdom has a king. It wouldn't be a kingdom without it. Jesus is the King of this holy nation. This has immense implications for someone who feels pursued and pressured. We usually think about Jesus' persecution as being the cross and the torments leading up to it. But I can't help but remember probably the easiest memory verse ever given to a Sunday School kid. "Jesus wept." Jesus has a characteristic that comes out time and again in the stories of His ministry. He is described, frequently, as having compassion, love, care, charity, and grace towards people who are struggling with issues of life. And we like to see Jesus as this perfect guy who can take it and run with it and not really show any effect.

However, Jesus was human, too. We see that side of him in the "Jesus wept" verse along with descriptions of Him getting weary of the crowds or going off to pray alone for a while. He experienced fatigue, He experienced the pressure of public life, and He experienced that anguish that comes from loving people so deeply and taking on their burdens. In other words, Jesus knows exactly what caregivers go through. He's not just a king sitting on a throne and dispensing rules and such. He's a servant who lives and walks among his people, sharing their lives with them. This is the kind of kingdom that those of us "put to flight" gain when we do our best to live rightly. We have a Kingdom where we are participating in the same sort of ministry our King does. And we can know, confidently, that He will take care of us because He knows our trials, our struggles, our griefs, and our burdens intimately. He's been there. He knows.

Because He's been there and knows, He sends people to us who have been there and know. My wife and I were constantly amazed at how people popped-up out of the virtual woodwork to give us a blessing of some sort, whether it was food, a ride, or simply just a shoulder to cry on. Jesus' body was (and is) alive and well in the world around us. It is amazing, just like a human body, that when one part of it feels attacked and damaged, the rest of the body will rally around to do whatever needs to be done to get things fixed and back on track. Just one thing I need to remember is that we individuals are a part of the Body. We are not doing it on our own. The Body is there to support and help out the rest of the Body. The Body is there to make sure that all parts are healthy and able to do their appointed tasks. If I am a toe, I can't say that I don't need the rest of the Body. What good does a toe do by itself? I need to be able to put away my pride and be part of the Body and welcome those gifts that are given to me.

It all comes full circle then. As I supported my wife, she actually supported me. And we have friends, neighbors, family, and fellow believers who supported us both through the whole journey. Perfect strangers lifted us up in prayer daily and even offeedr such small blessings as a phone call, an offer of a ride, or just a few moments to listen. The Kingdom of Heaven is an amazing place to live. When I felt like I just want to run away, I took comfort that I have such a place to call home where I know that, even though the shadow of death pursues me, God is with me.

And all God's people said, "Amen."

First steps:

1) Read 1 Corinthians 12:12-26 and pay special attention to how the Body takes care of itself. Verse 26 was especially meaningful to me, knowing that as went going through our rough time,

everyone else was right there with us. Shared pain is comforting in the realization that no one is truly alone.

2) Recall the web and pyramid of supporters I mentioned in the first chapter. Don't neglect them in your time of trouble. They want to be there with you. Seek them out and spend time with them. Let them know what you're going through so they can lift you up in ways that you may not even know yet.

3) Remember the humanity of Jesus. I can't stress this too much. We have a King who cares for us in the Kingdom to the point that He stepped off His throne for a while so He would know exactly what we experience. The best counselors are those who have gone through what we have gone through. Jesus went through it all, even to death. "What a friend we have in Jesus," as the old hymn says. Remember this and take comfort in it.

TOPICAL LINE DRIVES

Straight to the Point in under 44 Pages

All Topical Line Drives volumes are priced at $4.99 print and 99¢ in all ebook formats.

Available

The Authorship of Hebrews: The Case for Paul	David Alan Black
What Protestants Need to Know about Roman Catholics	Robert LaRochelle
What Roman Catholics Need to Know about Protestants	Robert LaRochelle
Forgiveness: Finding Freedom from Your Past	Harvey Brown, Jr.
Process Theology: Embracing Adventure with God	Bruce Epperly

Holistic Spirituality: Life Transforming Wisdom from the Letter of James
                                                          Bruce Epperly
To Date or Not to Date: What the Bible Says about Pre-Marital Relationships
                                                          D. Kevin Brown
The Eucharist: Encounters with Jesus at the Table   Robert D. Cornwall

Forthcoming

God the Creator: The Variety of Christian Views on Origins   Henry Neufeld
The Authority of Scripture in a Postmodern Age: Some Help from Karl Barth
                                                          Robert D. Cornwall
Render to Caesar   Chris Surber

Planned

The Problem with Social Justice	Elgin Hushbeck, Jr.
A Cup of Cold Water	Chris Surber
Christian Existentialism	David Moffett-Moore
Paths to Prayer	David Moffett-Moore

(The titles of planned volumes may change before release.)

Generous Quantity Discounts Available
Dealer Inquiries Welcome
Energion Publications — P.O. Box 841
Gonzalez, FL 32560
Website: http://energionpubs.com
Phone: (850) 525-3916

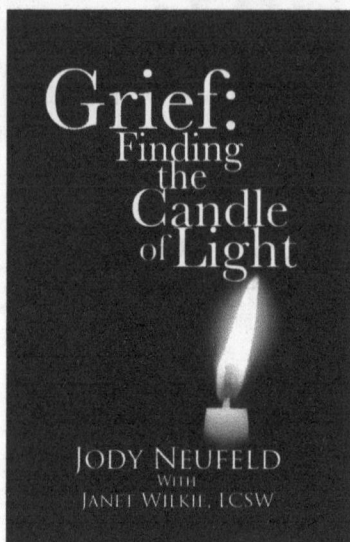

Grief: Finding the Candle of Light

JODY NEUFELD
WITH
JANET WILKIE, LCSW

I can say now that each road was different; each one had some very difficult periods, and yet God was faithful.

Jody Neufeld

What is the church?

What does it look like?

What should it look like?

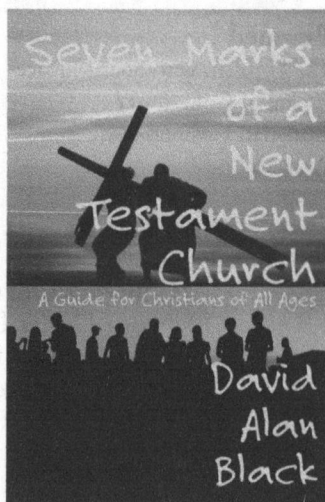

Seven Marks of a New Testament Church
A Guide for Christians of All Ages

David Alan Black

More from Energion Publications

Personal Study
Finding My Way in Christianity	Herold Weiss	$16.99
The Jesus Paradigm	David Alan Black	$17.99
When People Speak for God	Henry Neufeld	$17.99

Christian Living
Faith in the Public Square	Robert D. Cornwall	$16.99
Grief: Finding the Candle of Light	Jody Neufeld	$8.99
Crossing the Street	Robert LaRochelle	$16.99

Bible Study
Learning and Living Scripture	Lentz/Neufeld	$12.99
From Inspiration to Understanding	Edward W. H. Vick	$24.99
Luke: A Participatory Study Guide	Geoffrey Lentz	$8.99
Philippians: A Participatory Study Guide	Bruce Epperly	$9.99
Ephesians: A Participatory Study Guide	Robert D. Cornwall	$9.99
Evidence for the Bible	Elgin Hushbeck, Jr.	

Theology
Creation in Scripture	Herold Weiss	$12.99
Creation: the Christian Doctrine	Edward W. H. Vick	$12.99
Ultimate Allegiance	Robert D. Cornwall	$9.99
History and Christian Faith	Edward W. H. Vick	$9.99
The Church Under the Cross	William Powell Tuck	$11.99
The Journey to the Undiscovered Country	William Powell Tuck	$9.99
Eschatology: A Participatory Study Guide	Edward W. H. Vick	$9.99
Philosophy for Believers	Edward W. H. Vick	$14.99
Christianity and Secularism	Elgin Hushbeck, Jr.	$16.99

Ministry
Clergy Table Talk	Kent Ira Groff	$9.99
So Much Older Then ...	Robert LaRochelle	$9.99

Generous Quantity Discounts Available
Dealer Inquiries Welcome
Energion Publications — P.O. Box 841
Gonzalez, FL 32560
Website: http://energionpubs.com
Phone: (850) 525-3916

www.ingramcontent.com/pod-product-compliance
Lightning Source LLC
Chambersburg PA
CBHW011750020426
42331CB00014B/3340